PENGUIN BOOKS

Selected Poems: Micha…

Michael Rosen was born in Harrow in 1946. He studied Medicine and English at university and has been writing, broadcasting and lecturing since the early seventies. He is known mostly as a children's poet but his recent adult volumes, *Carrying the Elephant*, *This is Not My Nose* and *In the Colonie*, were highly acclaimed. He lives in Dalston, north London, with his wife and two younger children.

Selected Poems

MICHAEL ROSEN

PENGUIN BOOKS

PENGUIN BOOKS

Published by the Penguin Group
Penguin Books Ltd, 80 Strand, London WC2R ORL, England
Penguin Group (USA) Inc., 375 Hudson Street, New York, New York 10014, USA
Penguin Group (Canada), 90 Eglinton Avenue East, Suite 700, Toronto, Ontario, Canada M4P 2Y3
(a division of Pearson Penguin Canada Inc.)
Penguin Ireland, 25 St Stephen's Green, Dublin 2, Ireland (a division of Penguin Books Ltd)
Penguin Group (Australia), 250 Camberwell Road, Camberwell, Victoria 3124, Australia
(a division of Pearson Australia Group Pty Ltd)
Penguin Books India Pvt Ltd, 11 Community Centre, Panchsheel Park, New Delhi – 110 017, India
Penguin Group (NZ), 67 Apollo Drive, Mairangi Bay, Auckland 1310, New Zealand
(a division of Pearson New Zealand Ltd)
Penguin Books (South Africa) (Pty) Ltd, 24 Sturdee Avenue, Rosebank, Johannesburg 2196, South Africa

Penguin Books Ltd, Registered Offices: 80 Strand, London WC2R ORL, England

www.penguin.com

First published in Penguin Books 2007
2

Copyright © Michael Rosen, 2007
All rights reserved

The moral right of the author has been asserted

Set in Monotype Sabon
Typeset by Rowland Phototypesetting Ltd, Bury St Edmunds, Suffolk
Printed in England by Clays Ltd, St Ives plc

ISBN: 978-0-141-02455-4

dear e. love mx

Could I have imagined anything like
the sight of my father holding my
boy's hand, walking down the passage
and into the front room, to see a child
of mine in a coffin? Or the sight of you
and me sitting in the middle of the same
room, as this new baby shuffles her way
along the sofa's edge?

My mother told me that at the end of my first week at Nursery School, when I was three, she went in to have a chat with the teacher. How's things going with him? my mother asked. Everything's fine, said the teacher, but do you want to leave him out of religious things? Why's that? said my mother. Well, said the teacher, before we eat, we all stand up, put our hands together and close our eyes and we say, 'Thank you, God, for the food we eat,' but Michael won't stand up. He stays sitting in his chair, shouting: No thank you God, no thank you God.

It was their front rooms. No one was ever in
their front rooms. The curtains in the windows
were open but it was always dark behind. The
houses looked out on to the streets with their
eyes shut. I knew there were people inside,
but they stayed in the back. Sometimes I met
them: they were my friends' parents and they
told us not to go into the front room. I asked
my friends why not and all they could say was
that it was what they were told. I understood
that their parents thought other people shouldn't
see you as you sat down to listen to the wireless.

There was a competition in the paper: Write a
Story, and the best story would be printed.
I thought I'd go for it. I started thinking about
Solomon the Cat, a book I had read at school,
about how Solomon gets thrown out and goes
from house to house asking for somewhere to be
put up. I thought, I could write a story like that.
I called it 'Solomon the Cat' and I wrote how
Solomon gets thrown out and goes from house
to house asking for somewhere to be put up. I
sent it in and I won the competition and it was
printed in the paper: 'Solomon the Cat' by Michael
Rosen aged 7. It got printed in the paper's Christmas
Annual too. 'Solomon the Cat' by Michael Rosen
aged 7. Some time later we got a letter from the
paper saying they'd heard from someone who said
they'd bought a picture book about a cat called
Solomon who gets thrown out and goes from house
to house asking for somewhere to be put up.
– See this, Con, my father said to my mother. Someone's
   stolen Michael's story and made a book out of it – would
   you believe it? – the things people do – if I had the
   time I'd try and get hold of that book and sue
   the pants off them.
– No, no, I said, I shouldn't bother, it was ages ago.

My friends in the suburbs didn't know that on Sundays I travelled across London and walked by rows of terrace houses, greyed with years of coal fires. They didn't know that in one of these houses was a Bubbe in a purple cardigan, a Zeyde in a suit and an Uncle eating chopped herring. I didn't speak of the lav that was outside, damp and dangerous but though I could never understand how the ship got into the bottle on the mantelpiece, that was something I could mention. My mother and father in a picture on the wall too, standing in long coats in a doorway, arm in arm, younger than how I knew them, she with a perm, he with a chunk of a plaster on his leg. But what of the walks to the Bag Laundry with Bubbe kvetshing about how uncle Ronnie was cheated, she was cheated, I was cheated? Or Zeyde taking me to Hackney Downs, where men in dark blue suits like his stood around in a group? Say nothing. Say nothing at all. That wide flat open green, rimmed in the distance with the sooty terraces, and the men in suits standing talking, but not in English.

Bubbe = grandmother
Zeyde = grandfather
kvetshing = complaining

5

We would sit down to eat, the potato would be hot so I only put a little bit on my fork and I blow *phooph*, *phooph* until it's cool, just cool, then into the mouth: nice. And there's my brother, he's doing the same, *phooph*, *phooph*, until it's cool, just cool, then into the mouth: nice. There's my mother, she's doing the same, *phooph*, *phooph*, until it's cool, just cool, into the mouth: nice. But my dad. My dad, what does he do? He stuffs a great big chunk of potato into his mouth and that really does it. He eyes pop out, he flaps his hands, he blows, he puffs, he yells, he bobs his head up and down, he spits bits of potato all over his plate and he turns to us and says, Watch out everyone, the potato's really hot.

When we had ice cream, we'd sit round saying,
– This is nice, this is really nice.
But then my dad would say,
– You know what this could do with? Just a little bit of fruit salad with it.
So, next time we had ice cream, we'd have ice cream with a little bit of fruit salad with it and we'd sit round saying,
– This is nice, this is really nice.
But then my dad would say,
– You know what this could do with? Just a few chopped nuts on the top.
So, next time we had ice cream, we'd have ice cream with a little bit of fruit salad and a few chopped nuts on the top and we'd sit round saying,
– This is nice, this is really nice.

But then my dad would say,

– You know what this could do with? A few of those
   little tiny bits of chocolate scattered over the top.

But my mother wouldn't let him say any more.

– You're always the same, you are. Nothing's ever good
   enough for you, is it? I'll tell you something: if you
   don't like this caff, find another one. You know why
   you're like this? I'll tell you. It was that Bubbe of yours.
   It was her fault. She pampered you. All I ever hear is:
   'No one ever makes it like my Bubbe did.' Well you
   can get this into your head: I'm not your Bubbe.

And my dad would turn to us and say,

– What did I say? What did I say wrong? All I said
   was that a few little bits of chocolate scattered over
   the top would be nice. They would be nice, wouldn't
   they?

We roamed round the streets together but when we got to the end of his road he said that I couldn't come any further. He said that he wasn't allowed to play with me and he didn't want his parents to see that he'd been with me. So I'd stop by the United Services Club on the corner. By peering round the end of the hedge I could watch him walk up the road to his house.

Watching television cowboys was how they learned to gallop; *peeoo peeoo* (that was the gun) and they smacked their bums (the horse's back). We had the wireless: And now for our serial: *The Eagle of the Ninth*. It was the end of the Empire. Hundreds of Roman soldiers had headed north and disappeared. I ran home to go looking for them. At school we mapped the Queen's visit to Australia all along the classroom wall. Can you bring in pictures? No, there aren't any pictures of the Queen in the *Daily Worker*. And soldiers, please. She wanted soldiers; there was trouble in Kenya but there was good news: locking them up seemed to be working, she said. Hopalong Cassidy, Cisco Kid, *peeoo peeoo*, who are you?

My father said the army reached Berlin
and he was billeted in an empty house. On the
shelves were the greatest works of German
Literature – Goethe, Schiller and the rest. And
Latin. Volume after volume. The house had
belonged to a classics teacher. Latin and Greek.
Very neat handwriting, my father said. He mimed
the handwriting with tiny movements of his thumb
and finger. On the sideboard there was the man's
photo album and at first he was a little kid, then
he was at school and then he was in Nazi uniform.
Stormtrooper or SS. My father didn't know which.
And the man wasn't there. He was gone. For years
I had no idea why my father told me.

In the rough grass in the Memorial Park, where the mowers didn't mow, there were two drain covers. Someone said that they were bomb shelters and we made plans. One of us nicked a crowbar out of a dad's toolbox and we levered them open. There was a ladder and we climbed down into the room below. There was broken china and glass; earth on the floor. To one side were beds with blankets. Someone said that we could make it our den; I said that it was like when they opened up the pyramids and grave robbers had got there first but it was thousands of years before. And it really was ages ago, said someone, the war ended ten years ago, you know. Soldiers must have died down here, you know. We looked at the blankets where the soldiers must have died. Then someone said, what if we were all down here and it was our den and one of Sherbet-jacket's gang came by and shut the lid?

It wasn't only that they said a naked woman cleans windows at the madhouse. They also said that they met up with Old Man Harris in the woods and they wanked him off into a bucket. I was in the High Street and H said, That's him. But I was to pretend to ignore him in case H got into trouble with his Mum. He said his Mum knew Old Man Harris but didn't know about the wank stuff.

They also said there was a secondary school kid called Colin who met up with them and they went to the path by the field and jumped on girls. One day in the summer we were asked into the Head's study, one by one and he said did I know about what had happened in the field by the woods? I said no and later back in class a kid called Rafter got called out and never came back.

My father once tried to explain to me what
was wrong with their houses: mock-Tudor,
he said, phoney baroney – look at it. Each
one trying to look like something that it isn't.
If there was somewhere else better, more real,
more true to itself, he never told us where it
was. All the while he carried out guerrilla
attacks. He started with a builder's dump
which lay heaped up in a yard out the back of
our flat. Every Sunday, he raided it
for old sinks, lengths of tubing, plugs,
lampshades, taps – stuff that had been ripped
out of the houses he hated. If he saw something
out of reach, he would send me clambering up
the pile to pull out a lavatory chain or a
ballcock. It seemed to make him happy claiming
this stuff. But what made him really joyful was
when we went raiding empty houses. He
seemed to know where and when people
moved out. Around the fringes of where we
lived there were big, old houses, often set in
long, wide gardens; places that had become
run down and the people had gone or died.
We would head out on a Sunday morning to
find them. Sometimes he'd send me in to see
if there was anything inside. Sometimes he'd
come in too and we'd scurry about, looking for
things. I remember old armchairs, mirrors,
wardrobes, brown carpets. Places where you
could look out of the windows and see a lawn
and hedges. We took a torch and one time I
went up into the loft. Something caught his
eye. It didn't look much. He sent me crawling

across to fetch it. It was some kind of jug or vase. He wiped the coat of dust off it and you could see a dark-green glaze. It was a big pot with two handles, rippled, as if it had been made out of coils. Grab that, he said.

We're bombing Egypt. *Eeeeeeeowwwwwww!* Stuart
is wheeling round the playground bombing Port
Said. At the weekend, I'm in Trafalgar Square, fingers in
the fountain water. Britain Out Of Suez. Britain Out
Of Suez. They're bombing Egypt. But we've got Nye
Bevan. He's come out against it. And he's here now.
It's a great turnout, they say. Bevan speaks. Then up steps
Martin's Uncle John. His lips are tight. 'They've gone
in,' he says, 'the tanks have gone in.' They all look
at each other, scared and tired. It's a blow. My father
puts his hand through his hair. My mother rubs something
invisible between her thumb and finger. It's that bad.
I'm thinking that Anthony Eden must have sent the
tanks towards the Suez Canal. 'They'll be in the streets
of Budapest by now,' John says.

My brother and I were put on a train out of
Weimar and we headed off into the
Thuringianwald, a forest somewhere near
Czechoslovakia, I was told. My brother was to
stay in one house and I would stay in another.
It's all right, they said, there's someone in the
family who speaks English. My family seemed
to be some kind of farmers. Well, they had
chickens in their garden and I was put to play
with two children, a boy and a girl, who were
a bit younger than me and who kept saying:
'Kick me,' and running away. The one who
spoke English was a big girl who I thought
was as beautiful as a film star, tall, with long
blonde hair and a skin so white that it was
almost grey. She seemed downcast or lost.
Surely my big brother would go crazy about
her, but he seemed more interested in the one
in his house who opened her mouth and laughed.
I went to bed in an alcove, in a bed that had a
high wooden side. One night the big blonde
girl came and sat by my bed and asked me
about my brother and then sat next to me saying
nothing, looking at me as I had looked at a bird
that once flew into our front room at home,
something that belonged elsewhere now up closer
than ever before. She said that she hoped that
I was happy. I said I was. I didn't know why
she stared at me in my wooden bed in the
alcove and I didn't say that I had no idea where
I was or who she and her family were. One day
we climbed to the top of a mountain that they
were proud of and my brother walked along the

forest path ahead of me, strolling between the beautiful girls, talking in German while the children with me ran about under the pine trees, calling out, 'Kick me, kick me.' Afterwards my brother explained to me that he wouldn't be able to see them again. Not ever. He wouldn't be allowed to come and they wouldn't be allowed out of East Germany.

I nagged my parents for a torch:
– I'd love a torch, oh go on, one of those ones with
    the black rubber round them, go on, go on . . .
It was no good. I wasn't getting anywhere. Then came
my birthday. On the table was a big box. In the box, a
torch. My dad took it out of the box:
– You see that torch, he says, it's waterproof. That is a
    waterproof torch.
So that night I got into the bath and went underwater
swimming with it: breathe in, under the water, switch on,
search for shipwrecks and treasure. Up, breathe, under
again, exploring the ocean floor. Then the torch went out.
I shook it and banged it but it wouldn't go. I couldn't
get it to go again. My birthday torch. So I got out the
bath, dried myself off, put on my pyjamas and went
into the kitchen.
– The – er – torch won't work. 'S broken.
– And my dad says, What do you mean, 'It's broken'? It
    couldn't have just broken. How did it break?
– I dunno, it just went off.
– I don't believe it. You ask him a simple question and
    you never get a simple answer. You must have been
    doing something with it.
– No, no, no, it just went off.
– Just try telling the truth, will you? How did it break?
– I was underwater swimming with it.
– Are you mad? When I said this torch is waterproof, I
    meant it keeps the rain off. I didn't mean you could go
    bloody deep-sea diving with it. Ruined. Completely
    ruined. For weeks and weeks he nags us stupid that he
    wants one of these waterproof torches and the first thing
    he does is wreck it. How long did it last? Two minutes?

Three minutes? These things cost money, you know.
Money.
At the weekend, he says,
– We're going into Harrow to take the torch back.
We walk into the shop, my dad goes up to the man at the
counter and says,
– You see this torch. I bought it from you a couple of weeks
   ago. It's broken.
So the man picks it up.
– It couldn't have just broken, says the man, how did
   it break?
– And my dad says, I dunno, it just went off.
– Surely you must have been doing something with it.
– No, no, no, says my dad. It just went off.
– Come on, says the man, these torches don't just
   break down. You must have been doing something with it.
– So I said, Well, actually, I was in the –
And I got a kick on the ankle from my dad.
– I was in the – er – oh yeah – kitchen and it went off.
So the man said he would take it out the back to show
Len. He came back in a few minutes and said that Len
couldn't get it to work either.
– You'll have to have a new one, he says.
– I should think so too, says my dad. Thank YOU!
Outside the shop, my dad says to me,
– What's the matter with you? You were going to tell him
   all about your underwater swimming fandango, weren't you?
   Are you crazy?

Good things were a long way off. It always needed a bus and a train. Like for those New Years' do's where I was allowed to stay up and listen to Malcolm the actor and Solly the Communist councillor's jokes. What was so funny about Hymie getting lost in the Alps and when the Red Cross man came, him saying, 'I've given already?' It was a bus, a train and another bus to the place behind the cinema where they were building a theatre. All they had was an old tin chapel and a new hall they called the Stanislavsky Room. In the chapel I sat on my own, watching a play about a landlady and a man tearing paper. Then someone went crazy and grabbed him. A Jewish bloke got nasty. On Friday nights we would practise Stanislavsky in the Stanislavsky Room: mime peeling an apple, to show us how it isn't a potato. I had to grab a girl's hand and say that I loved her more than the moon. It was down to me to say that, because there weren't any other boys. It wasn't supposed to matter that I was twelve and they were fifteen and sixteen and seventeen and tried to be kind to me. Your eyes are like the stars, marry me, marry me in the Stanislavsky Room. Then out past the tin chapel, back on the bus, back on the train, back on the bus, the houses' eyes shut.

My mother said that she wasn't going to go on another camping trip until we got a better frying pan: I'm not going camping ever again with a frying pan without a handle. Whoever heard of cooking with a frying pan without a handle? If you did more of the cooking, you wouldn't want to cook with a frying pan without a handle. Everyone else who goes camping, goes with a nice frying pan, but when we go camping, we go with a frying pan without a handle. It's typical of your father. He goes out and gets a new tent, he gets a new lamp, he gets new sleeping bags but I'm cooking with a frying pan without a handle. I've sat there for hours and hours trying to fry onions, trying to fry liver, trying to fry bacon and eggs and I'm trying to do it all with a frying pan without a handle. There are good frying pans these days. I've seen them. People go camping with them. Not rich people. People like us. They sit there every night with their nice frying pans, having a nice time. But what have we got? A frying pan without a handle.

Malc's shoes smelled of fish because they
had been stuck together with fish glue. His
father had brought them back from Czechoslovakia.
They were, his father said, another
example of how Communism was improving
the lives of the Czechoslovakian people.
– See how resourceful they are, he said, using
   fish remains to make shoes. Nothing gets
   wasted.

At nights, when we lay in his bedroom – Malc in his
bed, me on the floor in my sleeping bag – we would
talk about the girls we fancied; and in the dark
I could smell his Communist shoes.

In the water they were very different, my father
keeping his head up, lying sidewise, stretching
one hand ahead, pulling with the other. Sidestroke,
he called it. It moved him through the water all right.
You could see that he didn't like being there, keeping
his mouth as high as he could, spitting. But my
mother rolled around in there. She could be lazy
with it, letting herself sink or rise, pleased that
her hair coiled and uncoiled over her face. Once
I looked down into the water and her eyes were
open in it.

My brother's girlfriends and near-girlfriends and if-only-they-were girlfriends were too much. They glowed in the dark. They smelled of lemon and cinnamon and rose; layers of it hung around our rooms for hours. They looked at us with sex-full eyes and disappeared off with him to his room, behind his locked door; of course it was locked, where I bet each one of them slipped out of her clothes and danced in front of him, driving him wild. I bloody bet they did, all of them, and they kept coming round and ringing on the door bell and standing in the doorway being ready. Until it went wrong and there was a bust up and I hated it and the girlfriend was gone and didn't come back. I hated that. But there'd be another one. Smelling so good.

When *Lady Chatterley* came out, the kid we
called Tails brought one in. He covered
it in brown paper and wrote on the front: Black
Beauty by Anna Sewell. In class, we'd say,
What are you reading, Tails? And he'd say: *Black
Beauty*. We'd say, What's *Black Beauty* like,
Tails? Good book, he'd say. That year, we all read
Black Beauty.

I ran away from home. I said, I'm going on
the Aldermaston March to ban the bomb. They
said that this was out of the question, the boy's
mad. Crazy. My mother said, Where will you
stay? You'd have nothing to eat, you don't
know anyone, what would you eat? You're not
going. Harold, say something, he's too young,
look at him, he's packing. You can't go without
a spare pair of trousers, how can he carry a bag
like that for twenty miles a day? Stop him, Harold.
What would you do in the evening? You need to
eat, you get ill if you don't eat. Take a tin of
beans. You can always eat beans. Harold, stop
him. There's the chicken. Take the chicken. If
you're taking a tin of beans, take two. He's
thirteen, Harold. Go next year, wait till next
year, they won't have banned the bomb by then,
believe me. There'll be another march. Go on that
one. You must keep eating fresh fruit. And you
like dates. He's always liked dates, hasn't he,
Harold? Just squeeze them in down the side of
the bag. Couldn't he wait till the last day, when
we'll be there? We can all go to Trafalgar Square
together. Harold, have you got the chicken?
Just because it's Easter, doesn't mean it's warm.
It can snow at Easter. Wear the string vest. Who's
organized the coaches? Do we know these people,
Harold? One orange! Take five. And raisins. He's
thirteen. It's ridiculous. He can't go. Keep the
chicken wrapped. Phone us if you need more food.
Goodbye.

H. M. Hyndman. The Origins of the Labour Party.
Essays have to be done. Hyndman? my father says.
You're doing Hyndman? Yes, I'm doing Hyndman.
A dark photo in a worn-out book. The SDF. The Social
Democratic Federation. Keir Hardie. The 1890s. All
that.
– Oh, you couldn't mention Hyndman's name in front of
   my Zeyde, he says.
His Zeyde. An old man in the 1930s. Maybe he knew
Hyndman.
Zeyde hated him from the time he supported the war.
He sold them out. Imagine: one moment all over Europe
they said they wouldn't fight and the next, millions of
them were dead. Thanks in part to Hyndman. What
else have you got? Stuff. What stuff? Chartism.
Chartism? What have you got to do on Chartism?
Why Chartism Failed. Failed? Failed? Chartism didn't
fail. What do they think they're doing telling you that?

We wanted to ask him what it had been like.
I thought he had stood alone in the school
corridor at midnight releasing the lever and
waving the nozzle towards the walls. In the
morning we sat in the hall and when we were
told how sad and bad it was, you could hear
Gad breathing. They had us up one by one into
a small room where they asked us about the sound
fire extinguishers make when they go off. Did we
know how that sounded? I said I didn't know. I
thought we'd all say we didn't know but Gad's
disappearance for several days suggested he
said that he did.

My mother didn't often shout at me but when she was fed up she would go in for long speeches during which she wouldn't hear anything you'd say.

– I'm tired of seeing you in those trousers, why don't you go to the men's shop in the High Street, what's it called, Harry Boothroyd's?

– No Mum, there's two: one's called Harry Reed and the other's called John Booth.

– That little man under the bridge, he'd fit you up with a nice pair of trousers, Harry Boothroyd, he's got . . .

– No Mum, one's called Harry Reed and the other's called John Booth.

– . . . he's got nice trousers, you look a complete shlump in those trousers, I'll give you the money now, you could go to that Harry Boothroyd tomorrow . . .

– No Mum, one's called Harry Reed and the other's called John Booth.

– . . . you could look smart, those trousers are a disgrace, I'm ashamed to see you wearing them, I'm sure the Stollar boy doesn't wear trousers like that, doesn't he get his trousers at Harry Boothroyd's?

– He gets his trousers either at Harry Reed's or John Booth's, Mum.

– So what's the matter with you? Don't you want to look smart? All this don't-care-what-I-look-like stuff, where do you get it from? – you don't see me going about looking untidy – your father maybe – but even he goes and gets himself a couple of suits from Harry Boothroyd's.

– No, Mum, he goes to either Harry Reed's or John Booth's, Mum.

– I'm giving you the money, here, go now, and don't come back until you've got yourself a pair of trousers, I can't bear looking at you another minute.

– Which one shall I go to, Mum? Harry Reed's or John
  Booth's?
– How should I know? I haven't heard of either of them.

shlump = untidy person

I am now doing what my parents did with
me: bringing up a child just a few years after
a son had died. I didn't know that I was
one-who-came-after until I was ten. Going
through photos and asking who was that
baby on my mother's knee. My father
saying it was the baby who died. My mother
never mentioning it, never saying it, no
conversation with her about it ever. It took
our child coming along, fifty-four years
after I was born, for me to realize that my
parents were people who thought about
how they had lost a child. It had never
crossed my mind before then. So, from
the age of ten, I knew that there had been
a brother before me, and yet I never looked
at my mother or father and thought that the
things they said or did might have been that
way because of what had happened to their
baby. When I was sixteen I went away to
France for six weeks. My father was going
to take me to the station, my mother was
leaving for work. She was going to leave the
house before me. I said goodbye to her. She
didn't go. She went upstairs to fetch something
and came down again. My father waved his
hand at me. 'What?' I said. 'Your mother. Go
to her. She's upset.' 'I've been away before,
haven't I?' I said, but really I was thinking
of my brother. He had been away this long
several times and there hadn't been any big
scene when he went. But now, from where
I'm standing today, I can see that he was

different. He was older than the one who
died. He came before. I came after. I went
to her but she said not to fuss, and she went
off to work. Not to fuss. And now this little
one. Look what she did today. She put her
hand in the plant pot, filled her hand with
gravel and threw it on the kitchen floor.
Don't do that, you said, and she did it again.
And again. So I took her up the garden
and she said, 'I throw stonies.' And laughed.
What happens now? Do we try to make sure
she knows that we don't want this to happen?
I'm about to go to the Turkish supermarket to
buy some hummus. Do we go through some
routine where we say that she can come if
she stops throwing stones or will it all seem
like life's too short, yes, just that, too bloody
short. Well, my love, you shut the back door,
how unlike you, while we stayed out in the
garden, and our little one was unhappy
because she wanted to come in and I said
that you were cross, there were all the stones
to clear up. And she said sorry and we did go
to the Turkish supermarket and we bought
hummus and when we got back, my love,
you and me, we sat outside in the evening sun
and drank cold Turkish beer. *Efes*. How he
loved *Efes*. How we're loving this *Efes*.

I thought it was the journey there that was worrying
her. I was the only sixteen-year-old she'd heard
of who would have to get themselves from London
to the Ardèche by themselves. I was the only one
I knew too. My father thought he'd make it safe
(for me? for him?) by running through the details:
Dover, Calais, Gare du Nord, *métro* to Gare de
Lyon, Valence, Aubenas and there you'll be met
by Mme Goetschy. There, that easy. Like holding
your breath till you get there. Like holding my
breath in the *gourde*, the pool in the river where
I'd met them all last year. Would the same ones
be there again this year? Benzizi the brown-
skinned midget? Goddemarre the Elvis? Maurice
the communist *moniteur*? Alice the Moroccan?
Mercedez the Spanish nun (not really, she was
fifteen but looked like that)? And the heat. It
would be hot like that again, wouldn't it? French
money, English money, traveller's cheques. All
to go in the maroon Moroccan-leather wallet.
– What's he going to wear, Harold?
– He's got his anorak.
– It's too small. It doesn't fit. He can't wear that.
– All right. He can have mine.
His? The East German anorak? Bought five years
earlier in Weimar. Or was in it East Berlin, where I'd
discovered *Bratwurst mit Senf*? I'd always loved
that anorak, with its soft tartan lining. Faded blue.
I loved that faded blue.
– And you can put the wallet in the front pocket.
  Then you'll know where it is.
Like Kästner's Emil Tischbein off on the train to
Berlin, but my money not like his pinned to the

inside of his pocket where the thief got it. Mine,
in the wallet, in the German Communist anorak.
Paris was hot. The Gare de Lyon was hot. Look
at me. Sitting in a café in Paris on my own.
Drinking *jus de pommes*. Out of all the people
from school I'm the only person I know who's
ever drunk *jus de pommes*. And I've gone in there
and said, *un jus de pommes s'il vous plaît* and here
I am drinking it. At three minutes before midnight,
the train groaned out. I stood looking out at the waves
of apartments and I thought of the thousands and
hundreds of thousands and millions of *petits pois aux
lardons* sitting in the cupboards of the buildings. I
thought of how school had ended with a coach trip
and sad snogging and I realized I had left the anorak
hanging from a door handle in the café.

I once arranged for a German boy to come and stay
so that my boy could speak some German for his
GCSE. He was a bewildered creature who blurted
out facts about America and reasons why boys
shouldn't clear up. He wanted to play with baby
toys. When I told him (because he asked me about
why I had a German name) that I was Jewish he
said that that wasn't possible. I asked him about
his name. His parents were Hungarian, he said. I said
I didn't think that that was impossible. When he was
leaving, we sat in the departure lounge at Heathrow;
we didn't look at each other. I saw a man, an actor,
who wrote a book about being a father, or divorce, or
both, and he was there with his son, the one he had
written about, and he was arguing with him about
what was in his bag or what wasn't in his bag and
then he said goodbye and tried to hug the boy. But
the boy was ratty and just turned away. Then I said
goodbye to the German boy and it was so cold and
he was so far off and looked so keen to get away
from me. I felt bad that I had got it wrong and I
remembered Mme Goetschy meeting me on Aubenas
station. Tiny Mme Goetschy, never out of her black
swimsuit, always tucking in the edges of her bum,
her side-teeth silvered, always on show with her
laughing and laughing.
– It's going to be a good *colonie* this year, she
   said and reached up to hug me and kiss me and
   hug me again.
– *Comme t'es grand*, Mike. You're so big. One
   metre eighty? Everyone's here. This year you
   can't drive to the place. Or walk there. You

have to go over the river. You have to pull on the
wires.
She took her hands off the steering wheel and pulled
on imaginary wires. I slid about on the metal floor in
the back of her 2-cv van, bouncing up into the
mountains.
– Oh it's marvellous you've come. You remember,
Alain? Maurice?
I said I did but there were always people called Alain
and Maurice. Next to her on the front seat was Jules.
Dark Jules, dark skin, black hair, long stiff neck.
Wasn't he the kid no one liked and there was a fight
last year when someone said that his bed smelt of
wee? At least that's what I thought they said.
Pisse-en-lit. It does mean dandelion, though.

The year before, my father had said that as
I had got on with them all so well, swimming
at the *gourde*, would I like to stop goofing around
with him and Mum and stay with these *colonie*
kids for the last five days of the holiday? He just
went up to the *moniteur* and said, How about it?
And a few days later I was in a tent making
lavender bottles with them all: bending lavender
flowers down into the stalks and weaving ribbon
in and out till they were tight, like, as they said,
bottles. The Ardèche was hot and dry like a desert.
The thyme went brown; there was lavender under
our fingernails.
– Make more lavender bottles? Who does he
  think we are, slaves?
That was Benzizi. No one spoke English. I had to
become French all day. And we did *Don Quichotte*.
Maurice, the communist *moniteur*, shouted at them
to learn their lines, make props. Sunburned Etienne
wearing a colander and wielding a broom was Don
Quixote, little Benzizi was Sancho Pancha with my
striped towel over his shoulder. Mercedez was the
beautiful woman. Alice was the narrator. There
wasn't time to put me in the play, Maurice said.
On the day before the show, he stopped everything
and said that he was disgusted by them all. They
were a generation of don't-carers. None of them
thought about the future, only the present. All their
ideas came from bad films and bad music.
– Your parents are all workers and trade unionists.
  They work their hearts out day after day in the
  Gerland Chemical Factory; they support the
  union and it's the union that's sorted it out for

all of you to come to a place like this so that you
don't spend the whole summer hanging around
with yobs. But you say you don't care. I'm
depressed, he said. I worry about what's going
to happen to you, I worry about what's going to
happen to France.
In the tent afterwards, Benzizi said that he was
going to organize a strike. Was I with them or
against them? I thought, how can you organize a
strike against a Communist? I looked up the word
for a guest. It said it was the same word for a host.
I said, I am a guest (or host) and I didn't know if I
could go on strike.
– *Merde*, said Etienne.
So I said that I wasn't against the strike.
– *Moi, je suis communiste*, said Benzizi.
– *Moi aussi*, I said, me too.
Mme Goetschy came down and sat on the floor
and said that it was sad, sad, sad. Soon everyone
would be back in Lyon, back at school, the
colonie would be finished. Let's not have a sad
end. Maurice cares about you. He wants you to
have everything in life. Not to be satisfied with
what you've been given.
– We're not slaves, said Benzizi.
– I agree, said Mme Goetschy.
We played *Don Quichotte*, lit by a bulkhead
light off the side of the shower-block. Don Quixote
and Sancho Panza tilted at cardboard boxes; the
little ones giggled and screamed. My dad had tears
in his eyes. Perfect, perfect, he said, pure Brecht,
pure Brecht. That Maurice, what a man, what a
man.

Pull on the wires. This year we would reach the *colonie* on a chariot. Everything and everybody would get to the tents, the shower- and the cooking-blocks on a chariot over the river. There was no other way. The 2-cv could go no further. You stand on the platform and pull one wire, while over your head the chariot's wheels ran round, locked under the other wire.

– *Vas-y*, Mike, Dark Jules said, off you go, and Mme Goetschy laughed till the silver showed.
– *Maman, maman!* (There was a baby on the other side of the river.)
– See! It's Mike, she called back to the baby.
– You've had a baby? I said. That was quick.
– Normal, she said. No faster than usual.

So I climbed up. Mme Goetschy and Jules watched from one side; the baby and Mme Goetschy's sister from the other. In the middle it lurched and invited me into the water. And I'm smelling all over of London – though this year I've got flip-flops and boxers. What's the big deal with these rubber slipper things you keep going on about? What's the matter with your sandals? my father had said. Yes, said my mother, sandals are good. Everyone wears sandals. They don't, I said. No one wears bloody sandals. I've got to have flip-flops. I must have them. This year I couldn't have the kids asking me again why I wore strange things.

I got to love the way the chariot was lurching. We would get up there in twos and threes, me, tiny Benzizi, Maurice the footballer, Pink Nicolas, and sit on the hot wood and dive or fall or bomb off it,

39

feel the rush of the water, over and over. We would
sit with our legs dangling, looking between our
knees; we would nudge and shove till we flailed
about in the air and smacked the river. It was
something we had to go on and on doing. You could
pull the chariot fast and fall off the back. You could
hang like a cowboy on a cliff edge. You could take
off screaming or roll off dead. You could sit in the
heat, pulling your sunburn off and dropping it into
the water, and talk about the girls one by one, every
single one of them. It was a place to be that was so
far and so long away.

I rehearsed a phone call home. All that money.
And the anorak. I rang and I told them about
how the journey was fine, and Mme Goetschy
was there to meet me, and this year we were in
a place by the river, we're in a horseshoe, we're
surrounded by cliffs, it looks like Lone Ranger
country; you can only get to it by a chariot over
the river and I left the anorak at the Gare de Lyon
with all the money in it. It was my father, and I
could hear a look. It was the one he did when he
looked across the room to my mother. And I
could hear her look back. And the lips. If things
weren't going well, they were both very good at
lip work. It was soundless tutting.
– You're not to worry, he said. If it's lost, it's lost
  and we'll claim it off the insurance. You make
  sure you have a good time. And write. Tell us
  how it is.
Mme Goetschy said that she rang the Gare de Lyon,
but nothing.

Benzizi was older and louder than me but he had stopped growing sometime when he was about ten. His skin was so brown that if he got in a fight, the scratch marks were white. The only people I had ever seen who looked like him were Brazilian footballers. He had learnt to collect guardians: Maurice the footballer, who also looked Brazilian, and Goddemarre the Elvis who had two sayings: *Qu'est-ce que c'est, ce bouleau?* Which I sensed meant something like, what's the point of this work? And, *Ça va, la foule?* How you doing, you lot? Maurice did keepy-uppies while he sang: *Allez l'O. L., allez l'O. L., allez*; Goddemarre combed his hair and straightened his jeans down his legs and word went round that he was seriously bad back home in Lyon. He'd done things. No one would say what. Benzizi was in love with Françoise, he said. He said she was the most beautiful woman (woman?) he had ever known. I thought so too, but I said nothing. But then, I had thought Alice and Mercedez were; they weren't here this year. And this year the girls wore a bikini that was like a swimsuit that had the middle cut out of it. All of them, apart from Nicole, who wore what looked like three tiny blue hankies. They poured Nivea on their arms and it was beyond belief to think that as they sat on the stones by the river, their nakednesses were only seconds away. I had never been so close for so long to so many girls wearing so little and they all seemed so completely, so totally, so calmly uninterested in any of us. They seemed to love each other, smoothing in the Nivea, washing and brushing each other's hair, painting each other's nails, moving each other's bikinis and T-shirts into the right place,

swapping jeans, telling each other what they looked
like from behind, going off to the shower room,
locking the door and laughing in there for hours.

This year our *moniteur* was Henri, who said he didn't believe; he had his beliefs but it was a long story. For the whole six weeks he wore the same pair of leopard-skin nylon boxers. He looked like a Brazilian footballer too. As he lay on the bed next to mine in our tent at siesta time, I looked at his hair. It was frizzy and crinkly, like a black lamb's. Alain the trainee electrician rigged up a record player outside between the fig trees, Benzizi played Les Platters, four black men who sang 'Sixteen Tons', and Ray Charles, who sang 'Georgia, Georgia' and 'Let me hear you say, yeah'. Benzizi could do a Ray Charles 'Yeah-eah-eah' perfectly and he said that I ought to be able to too but he left me alone while he jived with Françoise, who stood a foot taller than him. Henri interrupted Ray Charles with a jazz cabaret big-band singer called Léo Ferré who sang about a beautiful girl who he called *Jolie Môme*, beautiful Paris which he called *Paname*, and a hard-labour camp on the Ile de Ré where the men sang '*Merde à Vauban*' – shit to Vauban, who Henri explained was a famous nineteenth-century civil engineer. Benzizi rocked his head back, hung out his little hands in an Elvis way and sang, 'Yeah-eah-eah.'

Our tent stood on an old vine terrace where vines
still grew, and Maurice the footballer raided them,
grabbing the bunches, holding them above his
mouth and running his lips over the grapes as a
camel would, pulling them into his mouth. He
laughed at me trying eat them one by one, spitting
the pips out.
– Just scoff them, *bouffe, bouffe*, he shouted.
Our tent smelt of armpits, grit, hot canvas and old
comic books. Nothing covered the ground apart
from old duckboards, *caillebottis*, so our beds
worked their way into the earth. When we lay on
our backs on our beds in the afternoons, we'd
watch the sweat swell out of our chests, the beasts
run over the roof: the plastic-bucket-green praying
mantis stalking the flying grasshopper with a spike
sticking out of her rear, horseflies as big as your
thumb planning their next plunge into your arm, and
ants climbing the legs of the beds. What were they
all for, these things? Someone left a cigarette end in
the rubbish basket while we were hanging round the
river and it was Dark Jules (who, it turned out, did
piss in his bed) who spotted the smoke while he was
coming away from the shower-block. As he ran
towards the tent, it burst into flames and he was
yelling and yelling. He got there first and ran into
the tent and grabbed our stuff and threw it out into
the vines, went in and grabbed some more, threw
that, and so by the time we got there he was crying
and choking but he had saved a load of our stuff.
Soon, Henri the *moniteur* had a chain set up and we
were hurling water at it, and I was thinking about the
praying mantis, *la mante religieuse*, burned at the stake,

and hours later, sitting under the fig tree Pink Nicolas said that Dark Jules's sheet hadn't burned and the girls told Pink Nicolas that he was a shit and smacked him hard.

Mme Goetschy's husband turned up and said that
the boys from the union at Berliet would be joining
us. Berliet, the truck factory. That was why Lucien
le blond turned up along with two tall white boys,
Bernard *et* Bertrand. Lucien was white too but that
was because he was nearly albino. White wavy hair
that he was always patting, and white hairs on his
legs. He said he had won the Marseille under-seventeen
two hundred metres. He wore running shorts, and once
when we camped out by the side of the river he danced
in front of everybody singing Little Richard's
'Balambambula tooty frooty' as if it was French. He
liked the way his legs moved. When we were up
on the plateau in the heavy heat, he got thirsty but
I had brought my dad's US Army water bottle.
– Let me have a drink, he said.
– Hang on, I said.
– You shit, he said, call yourself a Communist and
   you can't share your water?
And he rammed the metal spout into my teeth.

Bernard *et* Bertrand said that they were the kind of guys who like to do things and Benzizi looked round at everyone. Bernard *et* Bertrand would have to learn that when it came to doing things they should talk to Benzizi first. They organized the building of a ford. Every day, we lifted rocks and boulders and laid them in the river. I had never sweated like it. M. Goetschy came and stood on the bank and saw my back looking up at the sun.

– *Jolie écrevisse!* he called out, pretty lobster!
We moved hundreds of stones. Henri loved it, he called us *bagnards*, hard-labour convicts, and sang '*Merde à Vauban*' at us. Goddemarre said, *Qu'est-ce que c'est, ce bouleau?* One day, after moving more boulders, we sat down to eat, and I think Henri said something about how maybe even if we finished the ford, we probably wouldn't be able to get cars over it and Bernard exploded. He shouted about how it had been his idea and that we hadn't helped him, and Henri had never taken it seriously and we could all go fuck ourselves and he was fucked if he was going to eat the rest of his dinner. Bertrand, who was the only French boy in shorts I had ever seen with socks on, put his arm round him but Bernard shrugged it off. I said if he wasn't eating his ice cream, I would have it and I pulled his plate over and sat eating his ice cream. Benzizi and Goddemarre and Pink Nicolas and Maurice the footballer and Alain the trainee electrician looked at me. I went on eating the ice cream.

– Benzizi said, we don't do that sort of thing, Mike.

Henri said that tonight we were going to
go up on the plateau and walk all night. We
crossed the river in the dark but there was
enough light from the stars for us to see
ourselves in the river. Up on the plateau we
saw glow-worms and toads; we alerted dogs
and got lost.
– We'll make a fire, said Henri.
So we made a fire and we cooked *petits pois
aux lardons*; he stamped on the flames to turn
the wood to embers and threw strips of meat on
them. We sat under a bluey-white roadside light,
eating. Nicole and Giselle said that we would
never get back to the camp and everyone asked
Henri if he knew where we were.
– No, he said, so let's go.
A few hundred yards down the road he stopped.
He got out his torch and shone it on a stone by
the side of the road. There was a list of names.
Henri said that there had been a village here and
during the war the Nazis had killed all the men
of the village.
– Bastards, said Benzizi.
– *Dégueulasses*, said Alain the trainee
   electrician.
We stood in the road, above us a huge sky,
the one or two trees watching us, Henri
at one end of a beam of light and the men's
names on the other. I tried asking Henri what
had happened but he couldn't speak and
Benzizi put his hand on my arm to shut me up.

I needed them more than they needed me. They
knew each other, their mothers and fathers worked
together, they shared the same schools and streets
and shops. They talked about meeting in the market.
I wanted to be them but I was irritated that I wasn't
them. There didn't seem to be anything they wanted
from me or anyone English that they wanted to know
about, or any English words that they wanted to hear.
They didn't need to know about houses with their eyes
shut, or why it got up my nose that the deputy head
had told me that her idea of the ideal grammar
school pupil was one who conforms and why the
ones who didn't, discovered Charlie Parker. My
currency was valueless. The joke about Hymie and
the Red Cross didn't translate; my imitation of our
biology teacher or *Danger Man* from weekend TV
didn't work. No one needed to care about even the
tiniest fragment of cricket or Arsenal. There was a time
when someone asked me something about Prince
Charles but I said that I was a republican, which set
up a running gag: every other day someone sitting
near me would sing 'Godde sev ze quinne' and leap
to their feet. I said that I thought Brigitte Bardot was
incroyable because the previous year I had seen her
projected on to a wall in the village square down the
road from here; babies crying, children playing football,
when in the midst of the kerfuffle, up there on the wall
for all to see, framed by the café owner's washing, BB
took all her clothes off and lay down on her back on
a beach. And the old ladies in black, their husbands long
dead from the war, the old men who had just finished their
game of *boules* right where we were sitting, the young
women who were making plans for the fête next week, the

young men who knew that one day soon they would
have to leave this place for work in Clermont or Lyon,
all of them, the whole village, clapped to see Bardot show
herself to them right there on their wall.
– You know, I said, they cut that bit out when they
   showed it in England.
– Ah, that's you Anglo-Saxons again, said Henri
   the *moniteur*.
And I thought, what have the Anglo-Saxons got to do
with it? What's he on about? And anyway, *merde, je
suis pas anglo-saxon, moi, hein?* Shit, I'm not Anglo-Saxon,
me, OK?

In the wood across the river the rocks turned
into a cliff. In amongst these was a cave. The
Grotte du soldat, they called it, because during
the war, which, after all, had ended only
seventeen years earlier, a man from the
Resistance had hidden in it. We went in with
torches, the cool smacking our faces; the heat
hugging us when we came out. I often did the
trip inside with Pink Nicolas. Like me, he seemed
to want the blackness beyond the pool of torch-
light. There was a cliff about twice our height that
we had to climb up. At the top, we had to lie down
and squeeze under a rock to get into the next
chamber and there was a moment when you weren't
holding on to anything; the rock seemed to weigh
down on your chest in the dark, while you remembered,
but couldn't see, the cliff below. Once Pink Nicolas
and me moved around the chamber for too long and
we couldn't find our way back to the cliff. In seconds,
every metre in front of us was new and the torchlight
wasn't strong enough to light up the chamber. We
thought that we'd find the cliff by moving to the
right, thinking we were making a circle. We didn't,
and it seemed like we were going further into the
chamber where we'd never been before. Pink
Nicolas said that we should turn the torches out to
see if we could see light. For a moment we stood
in the cold blackness, listening to our breathing.
Then we turned them back on and walked over
the damp rocks some more, till we heard Benzizi
shouting that it was time for lunch,

– *Putain*, where the fuck are you?
– Pink Nicolas whispered to me quick, Don't
  ever tell them that we were lost.

Two days later, me and Lucien *le blond* were standing in the river throwing stones when Françoise came running out of the woods.
– Didi, she screamed.
Didi with his thick, knotty legs was Mme Goetschy's brother-in-law and a *moniteur* for the little ones.
– He's fallen in the cave and he's not
  moving, he's lying in the cave, not moving.
  Il bouge pas.
I knew where he must have fallen. Down the cliff. Lucien didn't wait to wonder, he started running. He splashed out of the water and headed for the office and shower-block. I was caught, should I go to the cave or follow Lucien? The way to the office was rocky, what if he broke his ankle? I ran after him. By the time I got near the building, people were running back towards me with blankets and medics had been called, Mme Goetschy's sister was sobbing with big sad sobs. They found him lying on his back, his skull cracked. There was a moment when we saw him as they loaded him on to the chariot over the river, his brown skin turned to khaki. I asked Françoise if it happened by the cliff, but she had no idea what I was talking about.
– Why did you run after Lucien instead of
  going back to the cave?

There was a tree I found where a cicada laughed
all summer and the fat red ants worked on me
and my feet. It stood on its own by the side of the
stone path running from the shower-block to the
river. There were times there, on my own too, that I
let myself go back to the last day; the coach home
from the day trip to Coventry when we knew that
this was the last time together. Five years over, and
now one of us was off, he said, to be a fridge
mechanic, one a travel agent, another to art school;
secretaries, hairdressers and more study. As the bus
pointed towards London and night came down, we
were passengers on a boat that we couldn't stop,
singing and drinking goodbye. So we reached for
each other, touching and daring what had never
been tried before. The boat stopped, we climbed out
and went off, this way and that, in ones and twos
down the long roads of shut-eyed houses. Under
the cicada, I wrote someone a letter saying that I
couldn't go on with all that, with any of that.

With ten days to go before the end, M. Goetschy came to us and said that we would go on a canoe trip for several days, down the Ardèche from Pont d'Arc to the Rhône. I thought he meant kayaks but a day later a truck arrived and we unloaded fat-bellied wooden canoes. One of us sat in the front pulling, while the one in the back had to both pull and control. He trained us on the horseshoe of our river, shouting, *appel*, *écarte*, teaching the one in the back to do what I thought only Hiawatha knew: how to paddle a canoe on your own. Only boys could do this, he said, and Nicole spat into the river and said they could have done it, *merde*. We fanned out on to the river at Pont d'Arc, and we're paddling, shouted Goetschy to us, under this, the biggest natural bridge in Europe, boys. I was with Bernard and we were the last in the line of ten red canoes pushing along on water that glittered in our faces. We called out to each other, and our voices bounced down the gorge. At La Chaise we tried to handle white water with our paddles buried in the foam. At night we slept on thyme and sucked Mont Blanc condensed milk out of tubes that looked like they ought to be full of toothpaste. Coming round one cliff, two naked women kneeling up in a canoe skimmed towards us. Keep your eyes on the river, shouted Goetschy and laughed into the air. And later we sat under the Cathédrale, a pinnacle of rock, three or four hundred feet above us, with three spires and an eagle prowling round. Bernard, giggling during his turn in the back, levered his paddle against a rock and snapped it. For the last five miles to the Rhône, he had my paddle and I lay in the belly of the canoe taking the sun full on, like, I thought, a sahib. Lucien *le blond* cursed my luck. When we arrived back at the *colonie*, the girls seemed to know that they should be there to meet us, and they told us how brown we were and we showed them our blisters and they went back to their Nivea and adjusting each other. They had become even more beautiful and unbearable, the way their arms reached forward and away from their bodies making a space that we were never in.

I was never sure whose idea it was to invade their
tent. The plan was that we would come down off
our vine terrace, cross the field and get down to
the bamboo copse by the river which sheltered
the girls' tent. It had to be secret and the plan
was whispered all day. We would go after *le
repas* in the dark, when the *moniteurs* sat in the
office, drinking wine, as the mosquitoes and
moths fried themselves on the purple killer light.
They would think we were under the fig trees
talking about Les Platters but we would be flying
across the field to the girls' tent.

– Are you with us, Mike? they said.

I wasn't sure what I was with or what I was
against. What were we going to do when we got
there? What were we going to say that we didn't
say when we were with them? Benzizi said that
he was going to tell Françoise that she was a
beautiful woman. Bernard said that he thought
Nicole was the best and Dark Jules kept saying,
Giselle, Giselle, and shaking his head. We crept
away from the fig trees, round to the vine-
terrace, and then across the field. At night it was
clearer that the horseshoe of the river sat under
a high circle of cliff. It was cowboy country.
There were about fifteen of us, hopping over the
rocks and thistles, swearing as our toes scraped
the stones. And then we got to the bamboo: their
settlement, with their washing lines hung with
their jeans and T-shirts. The light was on inside the
tent but it was quiet. Not a sound. We looked at
each other. What was the plan? That we would
rush the tent? Then what? Benzizi pointed to the

path through the bamboo and we tiptoed along it
and just where it opened out into the space in
front of the tent, we saw that Henri and Mme
Goetschy were sitting, waiting for us.

– *Salut*, said Henri. His face was lined
   with false smiles. What a good evening
   for a hike. You should have told me
   that you fancied one more before
   the end of the *colonie*. We could have
   gone up on the plateau again.

Mme Goetschy said that it was sad, sad, sad. Soon
everyone would be back in Lyon, back at school, the
colonie would be finished. Let's not have a sad end.

In the coach back to Lyon, Nicole cried and cried and cried. Maurice sang, *Allez l'O. L, allez l'O. L. Allez.* Coming down off the mountains, Benzizi shouted that the coach was on fire. We looked down and the wooden floor was burning. There were flames round the bottom of Pink Nicolas' seat. The coach driver stopped the coach and pushed his way towards us. He waved his hand and said it wasn't a big thing, *pas grand' chose.* He stamped on the wooden floor and the flames went out under his foot and off we went. As we got into Lyon, they started cheering and the coach pulled up under the walls of Gerland, the chemical works. Some of their parents were there. Not Goddemarre's, not Benzizi's, not Alain the trainee electrician's. They were men now. I shook everyone's hand. Let's write, we said. Mme Goetschy said that she would take me to the station, the Gare de Lyon.
– You call Lyon station the Gare de Lyon? I said.
– Of course, she said.
After a while, I said,
– And when you rang the Gare de Lyon
 about my anorak and the wallet, did you
 ring this Gare de Lyon or the Gare de
 Lyon in Paris?
– Oh, this one of course, she said.
At the station she hugged me and kissed me and said that it had been a good *colonie*. And I nodded and nodded and because I couldn't say it all, I couldn't say any of it and then she was gone.

My brother and father were waiting for me
at Waterloo. In the end, you wrote good letters,
he said. We started to get the picture. You're
not as brown as I thought you'd be. Did it
rain? No, I said, it didn't rain once. For the
whole six weeks we had sun. I got into the
car, my brother sat in the front and I sat in
the back. Don't you want to know your
exam results? my father asked. He told me.
I looked at London. So what do you think?
he said. Not bad, I said. Not bad? he said.
Not one 'A'. Not even for English Literature.
My brother was killing himself sitting in the
front. He had been there before. The results
inquest. How he loved it now that it was me
in the dock. He sat there mouthing: not one
'A', shaking his head, doing the sad disbelief
thing, creasing his cheek like our father did
and then looking back at me and laughing
and laughing. Have you got a present for
your mother? my father said. Have you got
a present for your mother? said my brother.

We were evicted from our flat. A man who
looked like Danny Kaye bought the building,
sold baby clothes in Babettes, his shop on the
ground floor beneath us. He cleared us out.
He tried to be nice about it by saying that he
wanted us to stay and it was only his lawyers
who were giving us the heave-ho. On my last
day in my bedroom I lay on my back and
wrote 'Fuck off Babette' on the underside of
the metal mantelpiece. It meant a new school,
the different world of a single-sex, town grammar,
founded two hundred and fifty years earlier by
a Protestant brewer. A group of them talked like
I was the first Jew they had ever met, and so for
a while they wanted me to be the kind they thought
they knew. If one of them dropped a coin by mistake
on the floor they would shout, don't throw your
money about when he's there; or, better still, one
of them would *throw* a coin down and say,
watch him, he'll be the first to go for it. I helped out
by putting on what I thought they thought was a
Jewish accent. That way we could all get on.
Another group came over to the house, and they
asked me what all my parents' books were for
but together we got into Big Bill Broonzy, Sonny
Terry and Brownie McGhee, Woody Guthrie and
Dylan – or Robert Zimmerman, as it told us on the
cover. They asked me if that meant he was one too
and I said yes, but then, I thought, so was Babette,
though I didn't say so. I bought a harmonica and
tried to play it like Sonny Terry:

Down in the henhouse on my knees, I
thought I heard a chicken sneeze. Only

the rooster sayin his prayers, thankin
god the hen's upstairs . . . We shall be
free, in the mornin, we shall be free
wooo wooo

Marching across the Park to school, saluting
Sixth Formers, his moustache at the ready,
he had a special pocket inside the jacket of his
suit where he kept a tennis shoe to belt boys with.
You couldn't see it, but everyone knew it was there,
and sometimes on a quiet day, you might be head
down, a door slammed, a brief shout, the sound of
the tennis shoe hitting a boy's body, another slam
and it was a quiet day again. You couldn't even see
the outline of it against his suit.
– *Antony and Cleopatra*. You know, chaps, Antony
   was a military man, a man that men would lie
   down and die for. I once knew someone like that.
   I was in the Officers' Training Corps in 1933 and
   the Prince of Wales, later to become King Edward,
   came to review us. And do you know, every man
   jack of us would have been willing to lie down and
   die for him. That was Antony. These are the kinds
   of things we can chat about now that you're in the
   Sixth Form. Carry on.

We were trying to get from Carcassonne to Perpignan. A 2-cv stopped and the driver was a chubby man in a black woollen shirt, glasses. He said that he was going to Perpignan in a couple of days' time, why didn't we come back to his place up in the mountains? I asked him his job and he said he was a priest, a curé.
– Are you shocked? he asked.
– No, I said, I wasn't shocked.
He said that he was a priest in a small village up in the mountains.
– You might be shocked. In the houses there's no water or toilets.
We travelled up and up and up and then on to a plateau with the peaks still above us. We took a lane that wiggled across the plain and down a crack in the ground to a village.
– This is Espezel, he said. The people here speak patois.
His house was an old stone farmhouse, next to the church. Inside, he had a vase full of teasels, black-and-white posters of the sides of buildings and bas-reliefs from the cloister at Elne. He scarcely had any furniture apart from a couple of old wooden chairs and tables. He said we could stay with him and he would take us out to show us what life was like for the peasants in the high Pyrenees. For a couple of days he drove us out and around. He showed us the village cemetery and explained that for the peasants it was a fetish. Death for them is a cult. It's a carry-over from pagan times. He showed us some tiny fields of grass that were almost vertical.
– You see those posts, he said, the peasants tie themselves to those posts and lower themselves down so that they can cut the hay. Then they wrap it up in huge bundles and

carry them back to their barns, the women as well as the men.

Out on the road, we saw one old woman, tiny under her bundle of hay, just as he said, and he waved and shouted to her and she grunted back. The next day, he said he was going to go up to the lake, did we want to come? Dave said no, but I went. Once we were there, he said that he was going to sunbathe. Did I want to? I said, no, I didn't like sunbathing.

– Do you mind if I take off all my clothes? he said.

– No, no, you go ahead, I said.

So he took off all his clothes and showed his chubby pink body to the sun. I walked about, throwing stones and trying to catch flying grasshoppers. He said he was going to read some Teilhard de Chardin. Had I ever heard of Teilhard de Chardin?

– No, I said.

– You would be very interested in him, he said. He is both very modern and very ancient in his thinking, he said. I think he is very important for Catholics, he said.

I listened without looking at him and mooched off again. Then he put his clothes back on and said that we would go back now. In the car, he asked me if I was shocked that he had taken his clothes off.

– No, no, I said, that was fine.

As we unpacked *Candide* each week, it
emerged as perfect. What made it so like a
present was the way Voltaire gave us the
chance to make each line mean the opposite
of what it said. He became a friend of ours.
He noticed that kings command massacres.
In the midst of one, the tragedy of one of the
castrati had us creased up: ten seventeen-year-
old boys in black-and-green school uniform,
too big for the desks in Room 14, rain outside,
Mr Emmans waving his hands: *O che sciagura
d'essere senza coglioni*, Voltaire has the man
speaking Italian, 'O what agony it is to be
without bollocks.' A few weeks later I was in
hospital. When a car had hit me, my pelvis had
come apart. All ten of the *Candide* class came
to see me, strung up in a pelvis-hammock,
along with all twenty of the rugby squad, all
thirty of the cast and crew of *Twelfth Night* apart
from the guy who was due to play Belch. He was
lying in the bed looking at them all and thanking
them for being so worried and kind.
– What's like in here? they asked.
– Him over there, I said, is a First
    World War hero. He's in here because his
    bladder's packed up. He told us the one
    about how everyone's a friend in
    the army now. Call everyone 'chum'.
    Right up from the sergeant-major
    to the brigadier-general. The new
    recruit's impressed. He says to the
    Colonel, so if we all call you 'chum'
    what do you call the likes of us?

what do you call your privates? I
call 'em the same as you call 'em,
son, says the colonel. I call 'em
bollocks.
– And what about him over there?
– Oh him and him and him, they're all
motorbike boys, they've lost their
legs. Him over there got so desperate
to see his girlfriend, they let him go
home for the weekend. The reason
why he's looking worried, is that
she's pregnant. He keeps singing
that Frank Ifield song: 'Don't Blame
Me'. The First World War hero says
to him, there ain't anyone else to
blame, sonny. Hey but listen, I'm
in trouble. Every morning at six when
it's still dark an Italian cleaner comes in.
I had been saying hello to her for a few
days until one morning, I leaned out of
the bed, and let's face it she doesn't know
why I've got this hammock round my
middle, and I moaned out: O che sciagura
d'essere senza coglioni. I thought she'd
think it was funny, but she ran out the
ward screaming. The sister came running
in and shouted at me: What have you
been saying to my cleaner? If you've
said anything rude or improper, I shall
throw you out of this hospital. So I
said that I didn't know what it meant.
It was just a line in a famous, classic
French book that we're reading for

A-level but because it was in Italian
I didn't know what it meant . . . She
said that she didn't believe a word
I was saying, that if I said anything
at all that offended any of her cleaners
or nurses she would do just as she said
and throw me out. Then off she went
and the motorbike boys all said, what
did you say? What did you say? So I
told them but it was on condition that
they didn't tell Sister that I did know
what it meant. And they didn't say a
word.

After I was taken out of the apparatus that was
supposed to be pulling me back together
they sent me to the Garston Rehabilitation Centre
where I was given a navy-blue tracksuit. By
then I could walk, which was more than Johnny
could. He was fixing a light on the roof of
a factory when the scaffold tower he was
standing on began to fall. He jumped up and
grabbed the girder above his head and the tower
fell to the ground. He hung from the girder
while the others went to find a ladder but they
couldn't find one long enough, so they rang for
the fire brigade and stood down below shouting
at him, telling him to hang on. The drop smashed
his feet and legs in ways that I didn't want to look
at when he showed me. He slid about on crutches,
pushing his fat shoes on the lino. And at tea-and-biscuits,
when we sat in our tracksuits round
green felt tables, he told us how he did it with
his girlfriend when he went home at weekends.
For this, he was warned about language. 'Language,
Johnny, language.'

I went out on the playing field and tried to remember
how to run. I could walk and I could jump, but that
thing where you take off from one foot and land on
the other and then you take off from the one that you
just landed on and there's no break? That defeated me.
It was like the way you don't know how the back of
your head looks. I spent days doing the jumping from
foot to foot thing.

I had just found and eaten a melon. In those
days you couldn't buy them in England. Orange on
the inside, marked out in segments on the outside. It
had been lying by the side of the road. In a pile. I
cut it into slices, shaved off the seeds, ran the
knife close to the skin, chopped the crescents of flesh
into chunks and fed them to myself off the tip of the knife.

Then I hitched a lift. The car was full of lavender. Three men
on the front seat kissing each other. They asked me if I went
to '*boîtes*'. *Boîtes de nuit.* Night boxes? Boxes of night?
The one with the sunglasses said, 'Night club.'
– No, I said, I don't go to night clubs.
Then they saw a Fiat ahead.
– *Un Italien, un Italien, un Italien*, they shouted.
They pulled the car alongside. On a two-way road.
One lane a side.
– *O Italien! Italien!*
120 on the clock, kilometres not miles.
Even so.
– *O Italien! Italien!*
He wasn't interested. They dropped me off at Montpelier.
– *J'espère que vous n'avez pas eu une mauvaise impression
de la France* is what I think he said.
– *Non, non*, I said, *pas du tout*.

I came through the customs with my rucksack on
and the man asked me if I had anything to declare
and I said yes I had a big nail and a bottle of
brandy.
– What's the nail for? he said.
– I collect them, I said.
– Yes, but what do you do with them?
– I put them on the mantelpiece, I said.
– Can I see the brandy? he said.
So I took out the bottle and he said,
– You can't take that through unless you pay
  the duty on it. You're only allowed a half bottle.
  That's a threequarter bottle.
– That's OK, I said, I'll pour away the extra.
So I opened the bottle there in the queue and got
ready to pour it on to the ground, and I said,
– You tell me when I've poured enough out?
– Sure, he said, but the bloke behind me said,
– Hey, I could drink that. Don't pour it away.
– Is that OK? I said to the customs bloke.
– Yes, that's fine, he said.
So the bloke behind me got a cup out of his bag
and started pouring the brandy into his cup.
– Tell me when, I said to the customs man. You will
  tell me, won't you?
– When, he said.

There was a typhoid outbreak in South America
and they told us that we shouldn't eat corned
beef. Don't eat corned beef. Don't eat Fray
Bentos. My mother went to the cupboard and it
was stacked up with corned beef cans. We always
had cupboardsful of supplies. We must never be
short of food. Ever. Families of friends might
walk in. She took one of the cans down and looked
at it. 'Better not open that till the typhoid outbreak
is over,' she said. This went into the family
anthology: this is the way Connie thinks upside
down. But when I re-run her taking the can down
from the cupboard I catch sight of her looking
sideways. She looks at us sideways before she
says her line. And one of her eyebrows is up.
And it was her, wasn't it, who used to say, 'Ask
your father what he's doing and tell him to stop it.'
When I was seventeen, I come home late after
circuit training – chin-ups, bench-presses – and the
house is dark. No one in. That means it'll be down
to me to make myself a pile of honey and raisin
doorsteps which I'll eat on my own listening to Big
Bill Broonzy. But she's sitting there. Sitting in the
sitting room with her elbows on the table, her hands
under her chin, looking at a space just below the
curtain rail. She hadn't bothered with the lights.

My father said that he wanted to go and see her, did I want to come? She was laid out in the back-room, oddly high up, with a sheet up to her chin. My father went in ahead of me and stood next to her head. Her skin shone like an insect and her nose had shrunk down to a beak. I couldn't remember her. What we had, had turned into sitting next to hospital beds, mis-hearing and mis-understanding doctors – the test was positive? Oh that's good. That's bad? How are you supposed to know 'positive' is bad? The half-jaw they had taken away, the half-jaw that was left. The calf's-foot jelly. The paper sheets. The sound of doors being closed quietly. I counted the years that my father and she had been together. From the age of sixteen to fifty-six. That's forty. I counted the years that I had been with them. 1946 to 1976. That's thirty. I counted the months to go before I would become a father. Four. She was going to miss it.

Hundreds turned up. There were people here I had never seen. She had been theirs too, had she? And they had been hers? This is a life? People come dressed like they never dress; people who usually walk in straight lines walking round and about. But hundreds. So she was part of a lot. There were people here, strangers, who had believed in her.

At the moment you were born, Joe, the doctor ran to the window and shouted, Hatched!

Yes, I thought, just like a chick, you are, little chap, how good that doctors can talk like that. When the nurses ran to the window too I could see that they were all looking at a pigeon's egg on the window-sill outside.

Snow is the enemy. And frost. They come for
me. They work their way into my blood. When
I see them coming I barricade my body with
Damart underwear and fleeces. I sleep in a
cashmere jumper and double up on the gloves.
With no loo in the house, a piss or shit is
dangerous. Moving down the side of the
house on the ice lets the cold get into my feet.
Twisting out of the clothes lets the air roar in.
Sitting on the pan is a surrender.

The kidney test showed that there was something going on. Not very much, but there was a slight reading on the haemoglobin which might be significant, he said. The best thing I could do was go to the Renal Department.

At the Renal Department, he had my file
in front of me. He asked me what I had
been doing that week. I told him I had been
making a Schools TV programme with
kids from the Isle of Dogs. He said that he
thought this stuff about my kidneys was
rubbish and he pushed the file to one side.
You're hypothyroid, he said. He started to
get excited. I've got fifteen students with me
today. I'm going to get them in to see if
they know what's wrong with you. This is
great. Don't tell them what I've said, OK?
No, I won't, I said. OK, you lot, in you come,
he said. Look at this. He was very excited. I
was thinking about hypothyroid from my year
at medical school fifteen years earlier. I
remembered a page in Samson Wright's
Physiology. A before and after. There was
a woman with a round plump white face, like
mine. Then next to it, a picture of the same
woman. Her face was angular and bony, like
mine had once been. When was that? Ten
years ago? Twelve? I sat and waited for the
students as the years ran over me, and my
eyes watered even more.

The students stood round me. It's his
kidneys, sir. He's got renal failure, sir.
What? he shouted. Kidneys? Just
because we're on the Renal Unit here
doesn't mean that he must necessarily
have kidney failure. You haven't done
the basics, have you? Pulse rate, reflexes,
temperature. You haven't even felt his
skin. Do you know, if you had done those
four tests, you would know what he's got.
Look at this. He bashed my knee with
the rubber hammer. No reflex whatsoever.
Feel this. He put his hand on my cheek.
Cold and clammy, he said. Feel his pulse
rate. Ridiculously low. And look at his
eyelids. Have you ever seen eyelids like
that? So what do you think he's got?
Some kind of renal problem, sir? No,
he's hypothyroid. Look at the myxoedema
on his ankles. He's only 34, you know.
Can you stand up, Mr Rosen? Will you
please walk along the line of the carpet,
putting one foot in front of another. I
tried to walk along the line of the carpet,
putting one foot in front of another. I
couldn't.

A week later I was back for the results of the blood test. This time I was with Dr Gesundheit from New York. Is your name really Gesundheit? I said. Yes, he said. Where did you get it from? I got it at about the same time as I got my genes, he said. Now let's look at your results. He turned the page over. Technically you're dead, he said. And if you're not dead, you should be in a torpor. They shouldn't have sent you home last week. Not only are you not producing any thyroxine, but the antibodies that destroyed your thyroid aren't there either. You're running on no thyroid, like a car running on no gas. You have to come in now. Right now. I'm going to order you a bed in the Metabolic Unit.

The news was that the same cells that
had been digesting bacteria were
now digesting me. I was being consumed
from inside. The cells that were so good at
identifying alien organisms – ones that
had arrived through the usual holes:
mouth, nose, cuts and the like – had now
identified part of me as alien too. Did this
mean that they had tolerated me for twenty
years and then suddenly found me undesirable
and dangerous? Was it something I did? Or
was it the cells that changed? Previously
content, doing what they did best, but then
came under some influence which altered
their attitude and so started to eat me?

Now it seems they've stopped. It was only
one bit of me they were after. I had expected
that they would go on finding areas to consume
but they've left off. Part of me has gone but the
rest is still there. It seems as if it is possible
for them to start up again, finding new bits to
ingest and eliminate. I'll say that differently: it
seems as if it's possible for me to start up again,
finding new bits of me to ingest and eliminate.
Once, when we were camping, and stuck in the
tent for too long, we wondered if it was true that
someone had survived by chopping off his hand
and eating it.

I was in a room with Charlie. His tongue
was too big to fit in his mouth. And in the
corner was a kid. I thought it was a kid.
It turned out he was a man but he was still
a kid. There was a group area with the TV
and there was a man who barked. Dog Man.
He was seven foot tall and his head hung
down on his chest, his arms hung low,
right down by his side. There was Ball Lady.
She was completely round. Really two balls.
One round bald head, on a round body, no
neck. You look bad, they said to me. You
look like a corpse. You sound like it too,
they said. You sound like you're talking
from underground. And you're cold like
a corpse too. You're the Dead Man, man.

I emerged. An old me came out of the Dead Man. Every day, I saw the face and hands and ankles shrink. I heard my voice speed up and rise. My lips shrank. I could move my tongue quicker and I unfroze. After ten years of being cold I wasn't cold any more. Charlie and Dog Man and Ball Lady and the kid who wasn't a kid were excited. It's all so quick, they said.

On trains, we'd play the how-will-we-get-home? game.
– I'll fly like a rocket, Eddie would say.
– I'll roll up so small, I'll slip into the telephone wires and
   zip back to London, I'd say.
– I'll fly like a bird, he'd say.
When we were home, we played the how-did-we-say-we
would-get-home? game.
– I said I'd fly like a rocket, what did you say, Dad?
– I said I'd roll up so small, I'd slip into the telephone wires
and zip back to London.
I wondered what it was about the game that he needed to
go on and on playing it but then once, we got on a train and
I said,
– Do you want to play the how-will-we-get-home? game?
– No, he said, but we can if you want to.
So we played it.

There were times when I was on my own
in the studio late at night. Through the
glass the producer and the studio manager
talking to each other with no sound reaching
me. They told me I was recording for the
world. Reading words from inside a silent
room that could be heard anywhere. Someone
once told me that there used to be a swimming
pool in here and behind a curtain there was
a grand piano. Upstairs and outside, the buses
curved round the Aldwych or streamed up
Kingsway; theatres gobbled up queues. I was
talking about books. The two women behind
the glass moved like surgeons from console to
tape to deck. Great writers fell out of my
mouth. I coughed. Go back. Redo that para.
Centuries pass. Tom Paine, Amy Tan, that
sort of thing. And then nothing. I go into the
operating theatre. The surgeons look up and
nod. I back out. Don't want to breathe on the
tape. Coming out, I hope Security don't notice.
Oh no, they have. 'One moment, sir. Why have
you been in there?' 'I don't know.' Outside,
the buses are racing. The drivers know where
they're going. The 4 from Waterloo to Finsbury
Park.

Thirty years later I arrived in the Ardèche with
my son and step-daughter. We drove down to the
turn on the road that led to the river. It's just down
here, I said. But it wasn't *just* down there. It was a
long way down and all along by the river on the
valley floor were campsites, the permanent kind,
with showers and shops. As we got near to the end
of the valley where I was waiting to see the horseshoe
and the cliffs I was gearing myself up that this too
would have its campsite selling *merguez et frites*.
But no, the tents ended and, just as it was, thirty years
before: nothing but the cliffs, the dust, the stones,
the scrub, a few vines, the heat in your eyes and the
river. Dad's going off on one, my son said. One wire
was there. Not two, no chariot. We can swim in this,
I said, and we can walk across. They didn't know why.
I had never said much about the *colonie*. It was
something in me. We swam across. I was shouting.
This is the terrace where our tent was. The house
where they set up an office was empty and beginning
to tumble. I pushed in an old door down below and the
pipes for the showers were still on the wall. The peasant's
house was going under creepers and out the back the
fig trees had spread wide and low. I tried to find the
path down to the bamboo copse but it was overgrown,
I found the way to the *Grotte du soldat* but my kids said,
Don't go in. We swam again in the river and I was glad
they were there to see it. I wasn't on my own. They
were nearly the same age as I was then. I wondered how
many of the *colonie* had kids. Had they brought them
here? Pink Nicolas, Goddemarre, Dark Jules, Bernard
et Bertrand, Françoise, Mme Goetschy, M. Goetschy,
Lucien *le blond*, Maurice the footballer, Mme

Goetschy's sister and her husband, Nicole, Henri the *moniteur*, Giselle, Alain the trainee electrician and Benzizi. And Benzizi. Of course, Benzizi. Not one of them had I ever seen again but all of them still there. *Merde à Vauban.*

I was in an airport at three in the morning
and a man was selling flags: Australia,
Nigeria, Great Britain, Hong Honk.
– I said, Excuse me, I don't want to be
   rude, but shouldn't that say Hong Kong?
– It does say Hong Kong, he said.
– Well, actually, it says Hong Honk,
   I said.
– No, it doesn't, he said.
– Look, I said, I don't mind either way.
– Do you want the flag? he said.
– No, I don't, I said.
– Well there you are, he said.

I got a summons. It said I had been selling Chanel No 5 on the pavement in Oxford Street. I wrote back saying they'd got the wrong bloke. I haven't ever stood in Oxford Street selling Chanel No 5. They wrote to say I would have to be in court. I sent them a biog taken from a publicity file and I told them I could get a letter from someone saying that I don't sell Chanel No 5 on Oxford Street. They wrote to say I had to be in court. In court the lawyer for the council said I had been caught in Oxford Street selling Chanel No 5. I said I didn't need to sell Chanel No 5 in Oxford Street, I do other stuff. The magistrate said that it said on the charge that it was me that had been caught selling Chanel No 5 and hadn't I received the summons at my address; could I confirm that? Yes, I could confirm that. And that is your name? Yes, that is my name. So, she said, wasn't it reasonable to believe that it was you who had been selling Chanel No 5 on Oxford Street? I said, isn't it his job to prove that it was me selling Chanel No 5 in Oxford Street? She said, the man who claims to have apprehended you isn't here. You said that it wasn't you selling Chanel No 5 in Oxford Street, can you prove that? And I said that I wasn't sure that it was down to me to prove that I'm me. Even if it was down to me, I wasn't sure that I could prove that I was me.

I went to see my father's cousin, Michael, born in
Poland. The story we had been told was that when
the Nazis came in the west, his parents put him on
a train going east and he never saw them again. When
the Russians came in the east, he was arrested, put on
a train and sent to a Russian camp. When the Russians
came into the war, he joined the Polish Free Army,
fought with them round the edge of Europe, finishing
up at Monte Cassino. With three addresses on him – the
cousins in France, England and the US – he chose my
father's sister's place in England. When I went to see
him, he wouldn't tell me any of this. When he went
out of the room, his wife said that he can't bear to
talk about any of it. When he came back into the room,
he said, Tell him the story about my cousin Leosia. So
they told me the story about cousin Leosia: When
the Nazis came in the west, Leosia pretended to be
a Christian. She put a crucifix round her neck, and
then she fetched her grandmother's brooch and took
the diamonds off it. She took the soles off her shoes
and put the diamonds inside the heels. She thought if
there were going to be any problems, she'd be able to
sell them. Then she went west into Germany. In Germany
she worked in a factory. No one ever found out that
she was Jewish. At the end of the war, she couldn't face
going back to Poland. Her parents, all her friends and
relations had died in the camps. She went to Israel to
find her brother Naftali. She told him how she had
lived right through the war with diamonds in the
heels of her shoes.
– I always knew, if ever I got into difficulty, she said,
   I could have sold them – and here they are.

– Naftali said, Where did you get the diamonds
from?
– And Leosia said, From our grandmother's brooch.
– So Naftali said, Listen, many years ago, Grandmother
wrote to me, saying that Grandfather's business wasn't
going too well, and so to help out, she was going to take
the diamonds off her brooch and put in glass ones instead.
Then she sold off the diamonds. She didn't tell anyone
about it but she wrote to me to get it off her chest. You
went through the whole war with bits of glass in the
heels of your shoes.
We sat thinking about it and someone in the room said,
– It just goes to show what you can do with a bit of
confidence.

We were on our way to San José or on the Santa
Monica thing when Ringelblum said he thought
things were looking good for me but he had
messed up. All he had in his fridge were bowls of
polenta and tiny boxes of Sun-Maid raisins. His
daughter picked when she came to stay and we
went to an old green pool to watch her train for
the college swimming team. Then his son turned
up too. There was some kind of trouble with his
talking. It came out in lumps.
– I messed up, Ringelblum said, but I've got someone in
   Michigan. You though, you're doing good.
– Well, I said, maybe, but sometimes I wonder if
   I'm crazy trying to support seven people on what I do.
– That's the world's first McDonald's there, he said. You
   can buy jeans for 20 dollars at Crazy Joe's.
– You know what I like? I said. Going round the corner
   to Noah's, buying a cinnamon bagel, crossing the street,
   buying a magazine, and sitting right there and eating
   the bagel, and reading the magazine.
   Ringelblum said, I could make it work for you out here.
   Does your wife like it here?
– She loves it. She bust her kishkes to come here in the 70s.
– I never heard that. Kishkes I heard. Bust your kishkes –
   that I never heard.
I needed him to take me to a kids' bookstore to buy *The Old
Woman Who Lived in a Vinegar Bottle* for her. It was a joke
between her and me about her always wanting more.
When I got back to England she wasn't there. Said she
got held up. It was lies. She was seeing someone else.
On the phone Ringelblum said he sounds like an asshole.
But she told me she likes assholes, I said. Told me six
months ago. I thought she meant me.

kishkes = guts   93

It didn't seem possible to solve things by doing nothing so I went to a flat on the second floor in Hammersmith. The limescale in the bath was stained with iron. The trucks going west and east listened in. I said that I felt that I was losing things but that people thought they were losing me. Was that my problem or other people's problems? he said. I don't know, I said. It wasn't his job to tell me, he said, but how interesting that I had expressed it like that: as a problem. That's interesting? I said. There was my shower that needed fixing; is that a problem? I said. He couldn't say. It'll be a problem until the guy comes and fixes it, I said, he's not coming till next Tuesday. You keep saying the word 'fix', he said. Are you saying that I'm in a fix? I said. I'm not saying anything, he said. Or that I'm fixed in my ideas, I said. Who can say? he said. Or that I like things to feel fixed? Or that I get stuck on one thing? Fixed? It's you saying all these things, he said, not me. Excuse me, I said, have you got a book under the table? Sorry? he said. It seems like this conversation is going on while you're reading a book and you keep looking up the things I'm saying in an index at the back. Wouldn't it be easier to just tell me what you're looking up and read out what it says? Either that or just give me the book? I think you need to think why you imagine I have a book, he said. I don't need to think about that at all, I said. Then you don't understand how we can proceed, he said. Then I won't proceed, I said. That would be a mistake, he

said. That's the first and only time you've expressed an opinion, I said, wouldn't you say that that was interesting? I don't think so, he said. And isn't it interesting that you've used the word 'mistake'?
I can say, he said, that it's a mistake because we've barely scratched the surface here, we need to go deeper into the forest before we can get out of it.

A complicated structure collapsed. The step- and half-brothers and sisters headed off in different directions.
For ten weeks, on the days when he was due to come to me, I said he could either stay in his first home or in the house I had fled, but he came to where I was, kipping on the floor of my office, a cold ex-stable at the end of the garden. Boiling potatoes on an electric ring was making the books mouldy. He explained to me how I was wasting my time bothering with all those phone calls. Then it was lights out, blow-heaters off.
– You OK, Eddie?
– Yup. You, Dad?
– Yup.
In the mornings he had to step over me to get to school.

I was sitting on the 253. The man across the aisle
was explaining to a woman that Jews eat people.
– I'm Jewish, I said, and I don't eat
   people. Look, I'm not eating you.
– He said, Don't you know your history?
   You should do some reading.

I packed my books into fruit boxes. Boxes for
peaches, grapefruit and avocados. In the morning
all my books had turned into fruit. The two
volumes of the *Shorter Oxford Dictionary* were
plump pears. A book I've had since school, *The
Pageant of Modern Poetry*, had become a banana.
Squeezed up against each other, books I've
looked after for years, travelling with me
from flat to flat, house to house, rolling around,
bumping up against each other, or snuggling
up to the cardboard walls of the boxes.

In days they would blacken and rot, unless
I chose to eat them. Sit there for hours
munching my library till I was fat and sick.

The last night together. He lay on the sofa where
he loved to lie. He was feeling groggy he said. Didn't
watch TV. Tired as usual, I thought. So hard to
wind down after evening work, I thought. Staying
up late, seeing his Melissa. Kipping during the
day on the sofa here with me. He got up once to
check his Pager. Melissa was buzzing him. He seemed
fed up, aching. Just like his sister had the night before.
Lying just where she had been lying. Temperature, aching.
– Hey, I said, a book of riddles has come through the post.
  They wrote round a set of poets and asked each of us to
  write a riddle. I wrote one.
  I read it to him.
– Do you get it?
– Yes, he said, your bum.
– That's it, I said.

Your bum.
Yes, those were his last words.

There were ways of figuring how big he got.
Like where his eyes came to, face to face.
The way his finger-tips edged beyond mine,
hand to hand. His wrists peering out of
the ends of his shirtsleeves. The way the guys
couldn't keep hold of his body bag as they
tried to slide it down the stairs.

It wasn't a good idea to leave him in the morgue.
He came back to the house and people went in
to see him. His hair was still growing. A short
blond fuzz came out round his hairline. I put
my hand on his chest and it rustled. Under his
shirt they'd dressed him in a bin bag. They must
have cut him about to find out what happened.
I mucked about with his hair. His shoes were
where he left them. His shoes are where he
left them.

Next door neighbour Rob works late, talks football, enjoys parties, goes running, washes up. He didn't drop in or leave a note. I didn't see him for several days. Those first worst days. Then, in the alley between our houses, I saw him. He saw me. We stood face to face.

– Rather you than me, he said.

We went on standing.

– And best of luck Saturday, he said.

I thought, but the funeral isn't on Saturday.

– And he said, Arsenal playing Spurs.

There's a way we make it the loneliest moment
of all. Even our eyes are supposed to look inwards.
Dr Dave, who'd known him since he was a funny
fat baby, said he'd've drifted off, losing it without
knowing it. In the days around then, someone left
bags full of nails in markets, in a pub, with explosive
packed in to shoot the nails out. It worked. Others
were seeing their sons taken off in bags too. What with
it being Brixton, Whitechapel and Soho it wasn't
hard to figure the scheme. Sure enough, it turned out
that the bomber's head was full of swastikas and he hung
out with people who do what they can for the white
race. A high-up in the Met said he was acting alone.

I knew something wasn't right next door. Our side used to shake every time Wilma put her foot on the sewing-machine pedal which was about every ten seconds 14 hours a day. She was an outworker for C&As running up pleated blue skirts. He mended cars on the street. Fords.

The sewing stopped and Wilma lay on the front room floor listening to *Music for Lovers*. Did that for a couple of weeks then left with the baby leaving David with the three boys. He didn't understand it, he had done his best but what can you do? Then someone broke a hole in his back fence, came into the house, went to the wardrobe and went away with some photos of the family. David said he didn't understand why anyone would do that but what can you do? We broke up too. The baby died – I mean she got to be 18 years old and died. It was meningitis. We went to the funeral and then our baby died – meningitis – he was 18 too and they came to his funeral.

dear joe, your wild noisy huge brother
is dead. I couldn't do what my parents did:
bring two boys, four years apart through the maze.
I don't know if I'll find my way as well
as they did, seeing as they lost one
back near the beginning.

thank you for your card. I can't answer your
question: 'What can I say?' as I don't know what
to say either. You're right, it is a loss. It reminds
me that I lost him. He was there. Then he
wasn't. Though in between, he was blue and
stiff and landed with a thud when 999 told
me to pull him to the floor. Yes, it is unfair and
cruel. It also makes me tired with a
tiredness that hangs on like a dog. It's nice of
you to say you'll always remember him. You won't.

Hundreds of you turned up. I was a cork floating on you. Not a stone. Did I thank you for that? You made me bob. You were good.

One of us fell off the boat. Look in our
faces, read our eyes as we come ashore.
One of us fell off the boat. We're back.
In our homes, you can see that there are
times when we hate surviving. There
are times when we think how easy to
have been him. One wave and gone.

We're travellers on the road, always on the
road. Sometimes joined by strangers who
become friends who walk with us a while,
a day maybe, a year, maybe more. Then we
part. Maybe they've got another road to go
on, maybe it's us who turn off. Either way
we don't see them again. There's someone I
walked with for nearly thirty years. I was a
little thing, a tiny thing, when I joined her.
Then after thirty years she went. There's two
others. I've been with those two guys till now,
walking on. Here's one, been walking with me
since he was a little thing too, still walking.
Others, many others. One I joined when she
was just over one, walking along. Another, been
with us for thirteen. And here's one I met up with
when she was seven. We got through about ten years
on the road together but about five years ago she
found it easier to be up ahead somewhere.
I catch sight of her sometimes, we wave,
even meet up for a while. There's one who
left altogether. He was with us for nearly
nineteen and oh he kept us laughing on the way,
his jokes, his faces, his noise, he took up
half the road, you know.

In Paris where we went to find out what we thought about him not being with us any more I bought a card. It's from an engraving by Jean-Baptiste Oudry (1686–1755), *Les deux aventuriers et le talisman*, an illustration of one of La Fontaine's fables. A man is carrying an elephant – bending under the weight of it. He bends at the knees as well, head down, face to the ground. What's more, the man is trying to walk. He's struggling to take a step forward up a mountain. Above him is a rocky shoulder and across from him is an even bigger crag, overlooking him. But he hasn't fallen over and he's got that elephant gripped round its front legs. He's carrying the elephant. Jean-Baptiste Oudry has made sure that he'll go on and on carrying it. At least as long as I've got it on my noticeboard. He's carrying the elephant.

The woman in the cemetery in Montparnasse
is crying and she's crying because her son has
died, he's died in an accident and she's brought
him flowers and she brings him flowers every
day and she looks at the photo on his grave
and when she looks at the photo she cries and
she cries and I say our son died too and I ask her
when her son died and she says eight years ago
and I say ours was two weeks ago and she doesn't
hear but I think of her as reaching out to me to
join her to be part of this and I said goodbye and
here in Montparnasse I was in a place where
everyone was dead and I was glad of their
company but I thought I don't want to join your
death club, I wished her nothing but the best but
no, I couldn't. Look at you, Samuel Beckett with
your big marble slab.

Only us. That's all-of-us. All there is, is an us
until there isn't an us. Maybe it'll be one-of-us that
goes, or some-of-us, or in the end the all-of-us who
were once here. So, all that we've got is either us, or
not-us. Nothing in-between. Or out-there. It's an
us-for-a-while, then a not-us. In our case there was
one-kind-of-us, one kind of way of being us, and
now, with one less of us, there's another-kind-of-us.
When that hurts I'm better with the me, when it's in
some kind of us, even if it roars with being a new-us.

He lost his life
His life was lost
We lost his life
I'm losing his life

My dead boy once made a clock. Instead of numbers, he put 12 letters that spelled: How Time Flies. It fell off the wall and broke into pieces.
– Hey, how time flies, he said.

Here are the pieces. I'll stick them back together some time.

There was a joke he used to tell about a man
who had an orange for his head. The man's head was
an orange. That was the joke. The bit about the orange
came at the end of the joke. You only found out
that his head was an orange at the end. But I don't
remember what the joke was. And that was a joke he
used to tell. The man with an orange for his head. Then
I found a version of it in a magazine. So I pinned it up
on our board. But later we took the board down, and I
lost the joke. I can't find it anywhere. I loved that joke.
He loved it. But I can't find it. And I can't find anyone
who knows it. It's gone. There was a joke and now there
isn't a joke.

don't tell me that I mourn too much
and I won't tell you that you mourn too much
don't tell me that I mourn too little
and I won't tell you that you mourn too little
don't tell me that I mourn in the wrong place
and I won't tell you that you mourn in the wrong place
don't tell me that I mourn at the wrong time
and I won't tell you that you mourn at the wrong time
don't tell me that I mourn in the wrong way
and I won't tell you that you mourn in the wrong way

I may get it wrong, I will get it wrong, I have got it wrong
but don't tell me.

dear Bank re: E. S. Rosen's account, the a/c holder
doesn't hold anything.
dear Fenwicks re: your forthcoming clothes sale,
thanks for the handout, there's nothing to clothe.
dear National Blood Service, he was proud to have
given but he hasn't got any.

My teeth are moving round my jaw. On the bottom rack there's one that's come out from the right and one that's come out from the left. Between the two gaps are ten teeth. And now they're shunting round. Like curtains round a bay window. Each tooth, wedged in tight to the next has started to nudge to the right. They're all leaning rightwards and this shifts them round in the groove in my jaw. Like when we stood at football matches, shoulder to shoulder, belly to back. Someone began a shove and it would move through the crowd.

Barbara whose husband died in a car smash told me
I'd have dreams.
– They'll be beautiful dreams, she said.
None came for a year. Then they started coming. He
visits. He stands in his grey check overshirt. He knows
he's died. Once he said he was sorry that he didn't tell
me it was septicaemia. I said I was sorry that I didn't
know it was septicaemia. Sometimes he's at a distance
in the way he was when I would drop him off in Drury
Lane in time for the matinee. Sometimes he's been
close on the sofa doing his crazy hugs or lifting me
off the ground with all his massive indestructible might.

The old city behind the city is coming down and I
am taken through the rubble up on to
the roofs, through the attics, knowing I
am the last to see it. It's all coming down, but it
doesn't have to. It could stay. It doesn't have to come
down, it doesn't have to be bulldozed, and I'm on
my own in the rooms, looking down at the ground,
and across the rubble to the row of houses on the
other side, looking through their windows to
the open sky and it doesn't have to be like this,
none of it has to come down, none of it, and I'm
the last person to know.

It turned out that the baby was in hospital.
Alone. No one else was there. She was sitting
up in a bed on her own when we got there. There
was a tube coming out of her nose but it wasn't
connected to anything. And she was sweating.
Her back was wet. Soon after, the nurses and
doctors arrived so I said this doesn't look good.

And they said you're right. Someone mentioned
fan fever, the fever you get from sitting too long
next to an electric fan. So then they got to work
connecting the tube and doing artificial respiration.
It was tense. Could have gone either way. But
she pulled through.

Later I was coming away from the place
and she fitted into the palm of my hand.
The size of a teacup. There was a bad moment
as I sat on the bus with her in my hand there.
She went still and cold. But I blew on her and she
woke up, stirred and looked around,
eyes wide open.

Is this the kind of mosquito that buries its proboscis in your skin and releases a stream of bacteria into your blood that multiply every few seconds and invade every cell of your body working their way into the nuclei where they feed but in so doing release an antigen that breaks down the cell walls of every cell in your body so you end up drowning yourself from the inside?

No. There is no mosquito that does that.

This is the sick tunnel. People with tickets for the Tube are sick on the floor. Then they catch the train. But it's not there. The lumps and flob have gone. Sick-cleaners scoop it up and disappear it. The stink stays. It's always sick in here. A dog's nose could do things with this. It could write a Who's Who from the whiffs. He ate mushrooms. She drank tea. There's evidence from this one, the smell might reveal, of abandon, a wild night beyond the reach of office hours; evidence from another of despair, something about the days being relentless and overpowering. Sometimes it takes two or three retches to get it all out.

He said, I am a misfortune bully,
I punch you with disasters.
I slap you in the face with the awful.
I'm a death junkie.
Feed me news about the dying.
Tell me about plague.
I need to know about the hidden poisons
that come in through the window
or stick in the cracks of broken plates.
Even leaning on your elbows is risky.
I come sniffing round your way
if I hear of someone who's copped it.
I'm the president of the fatal illness association
and I will be at your side
the moment I learn that
you or anyone you know is in a life-threatening situation.
You will think I'm here to help.

I was sleeping on my own, in the basement
with the house above me – one, two rooms
and an attic above my head and now no one
in the rooms, it had come to an end, and my
head was lying where a fireplace had been,
perhaps the room I was in was for a Victorian
servant to use, the rest had been a coal cellar.
Now it was a basement room. The fireplace
wasn't there, I was thinking, it had been taken
out. A builder had come and taken it out when
it was turned into a room. But in the room
above there was not only a fireplace but also
a great marble surround with a chimney breast
that went on up to the room above and then on,
up into the attic above that and as I lay there I
wondered what was holding it all up. Aren't
builders supposed to put girders or lintels or
beams across when they take out fireplaces
and I tried to remember if that builder had
brought in anything like that and I couldn't
remember that he had. Which would mean that
the whole chimney breast running up to the
roof was resting on, resting on what? The edge
of the floor above? The ceiling above my head?
But that would be a nothing. I got up and
went upstairs into the empty room above where
I had been lying and looked at the marble fireplace
and my eyes went up the chimney breast to the
ceiling and there was a small crack running from
the edge of the chimney breast at an angle across
the ceiling. And another one on the other side. I
ran upstairs again into the room above this one
and looked up to the ceiling. And there was

another pair of cracks there too. I had never seen
them before. But then I had never looked before.
Not once in the five years since the fireplace
was taken out. In all that time, when the house
had been full, all that jumping and larking about,
and I had never looked. So I rang a builder and
when he came over we went down into the
basement together and he knocked a hole in the
ceiling and put his hand through the hole. I'm
looking for a beam or a lintel, he said. Something
to hold the whole thing up. Nothing, he said. There's
nothing here. You feel. And I put my hand in the hole
and waved my hand about and he was right. In all that
time there had been nothing there to hold it all up.

An egg in salt water.
– The salt water is for tears, the egg is for
   food, life and hope.
– The egg is in the salt water, he explains, because
   nice things should happen or promise to happen even
   in the time of tears. Our Sunday gatherings and remembrance
   banquets are eggs, then. And so, and so, and so is this
   oval belly that the midwife is listening to.

We make a baby.
The baby smiles.
We laugh:
the baby makes us.

We buy her toys
but she plays with shoes:
she makes herself.

The cat's ignoring me.
So I'm ignoring the cat.
Which means I'm not.

The wind has blown all day, the bushes
in the garden trying to tear themselves
out of the ground. Your old blue chair
that looks like it's made out of straw
has stayed right where it is, its legs
stuck in the lawn, but the parasol and
the cats' dish have taken off and landed
in another country. We didn't want to go
out with Elsie, she might have taken
off too, or some lump – a dustbin, box or
branch – might have hit her. She's old enough
to know that she didn't like being where
she was, but not old enough to
know or say that going out might make
things better. So we stayed indoors
and ate old Dutch cake and pitta bread
until, long after dark, the bushes outside
gave up the struggle. We dressed up and
walked round the streets, Elsie holding
your hand, me pushing the empty buggy,
through drifts of leaves and cartons and
polythene bags. The buses sailed by looking
like cross-channel ferries doing the night
crossing, while Elsie put one foot in front
of the other. We tried to work out how long,
well, really, how short, it's all been, since we
met in these streets, and now look at us,
walking our little *liebeskind* over the paving
stones. Then we came home and in bed
said that we would make everyone sing
I'm a little teapot short and stout, at our
wedding.

I think I know why cats eat grass. Something to do with them knowing that all's not well in their guts. So they eat grass, which makes them sick. Then, whatever it was that was making them unwell has gone. It's not inside any more. It's outside. Evacuated. This is not the same as the hairball. Eating their own hair also makes them sick but that's because they lick themselves. The hair just goes in. What I don't know is why cats put the sick where they put it. They bring it to our doorstep. You can tell which sick is from grass-eating and which from hair. The grass-eating sick is a pool of foamy sticky stuff with bits of chewed grass in it. The hairball sick is more solid. Food mixed in and held together by a wadge of hairs. That way you can tell which of the cats has done it. So, some of the hairy sick is ginger. As the sun dries it and the rain washes it, we're left with a skein of ginger hair. Like the twist of wool you find on barbed wire when sheep have pushed through. The mystery, though, is why the cats want to bring us their sick. It feels so like an offering, an act of kindness or generosity. But that doesn't seem likely. When you watch a cat being sick, it looks like they're trying to bring up their whole system. Anything could come out. A kidney maybe. Is it a way of saying they hate us? We sick on you and all that you stand for. Or maybe they think we're Mummy and they just do things like being sick when they're round Mummy. Because deep inside they know that Mummy will clear it up,

give them more dinner and lick them all over.
Either that or just doing what you do with
good friends. You can do anything with good
friends. If you were at a football match and you
wet yourself, a good friend wouldn't stand up
and shout, 'Hey, look, my friend's wet himself.'
He would just nod and say, 'Yeah, right. Yeah,
I do that sometimes.' Even if he didn't. Bearing
that in mind, I just want to say that the cats
are OK. They're good to be with. And that sick
thing. I didn't mean to draw too much attention to
it. I do it myself sometimes.

He knows we thought he died but he didn't.
Though now he is dying. The doctor's told
him that he is. I'm not happy that the doctor
hasn't said anything to me about it. In this one
tonight, he's unpacking, he's going through
some boxes and bundles. I seem to have packed
up his newspapers and magazines and he's
saying that he doesn't see the point of sorting
them now but I say that I'll help him and we
go through the magazines, saving some,
throwing others. Then, in the dark when I
realize it's been another one of those nights,
I lie awake next to you and your warm skin.

Is this how it is? Two watchmakers
Oskar and Martin Rosen (or Rozen)
living, says their nephew Ted, in a
rue de Thionville in Metz or Nancy,
weren't there any more. Ted, now 94,
remembers his sister Olga practising
French by post and a letter from one
of the watchmakers arriving at their
home in Brockton, Mass. But after the
War, nothing. Is that how it is? A tank
or a bomb; a shell or a bullet removes
two people? Or does a group of men
turn up with a truck – then it's a depot,
a train, a camp; cholera, hunger or gas?
Is that how it is? Two watchmakers in
a street that's in the way. Then nothing.

These nothings make it all so easy
for people who give orders for war.
Perhaps Oskar and Martin appear in
the sum of French deaths. Unlikely – they
were born in Poland – a detail
which made them eligible for removal.
Perhaps they appear in the sum of
Polish deaths – unlikely – they had left.
Perhaps they are in the sum of Jewish
deaths – not necessarily, it depends
who was counting.

So that's how it is. You're a watchmaker,
then you're not. Tiny springs, tiny cogs,
Tick, tock, tick, tock, tick . . .

Little bloke, hello. I saw you being lifted out as
you and your mother were saved and you've been
laughing ever since. You don't believe in falling
or staying asleep. In the seconds before you drop off,
you wave your arms, fling your head backwards,
and push my chest or arm or chin with your heels.
Then you're as heavy as a pudding. But not for long.
You do your own wake-up calls, often after half an
hour of sleep: you throw your legs up, open your eyes,
with a face that says, who did that, who woke me up?
It was you, little bloke, you did it to yourself. And we
say, it's OK; it was that thing called sleep, it's something
people do. When you're older you'll look forward to it.
For the time being we'll just have to take it, that you
don't think it's a very good idea.

I am peeling an apple. A Bramley's.
Eight of them. They sit in the water
in the sink and as I pull the peeler
round, the shavings drop into the water.
By the time I lift the last apple out,
I have to shake it free of green skin
and dug-out black bits. The naked
apples sit in a colander on the draining
board, waiting for me to chop them into
eight segments on a board. I carve out
the semi-circles of core and pips.
Then as I hold the crescents of apple
over a saucepan, cutting chips by
pulling the knife towards my thumb,
I am my mother. Water in, till she can
see it, a handful of sultanas, a chunk of
dark sugar and a cinnamon stick. Stewed
apple, my brother eating it out of the
saucepan. My kids don't like it very
much. But you do, don't you? Especially
if I bung it in a crumble.

Popping these white
pills out of their silver
cocoons. Two a day
every day every year.
Seeping into my cells,
all day, doing what
your thyroid does
without any help.
There under the skin
of your neck, where it
slides over your throat.
That's unfrozen me
again.

This is the man who leaves things behind.
Here is the bag he left in the house.
Here is the hold-all he left on the train.
Here is the phone he left on the bus.
Here are the people who try to find him
to tell him they've got his things.
Here are the people who sit with him
and hold his head.
Here is the thought that he doesn't
want to leave.